THE 100 BEST BRAIN-BOOSTERS

Puzzles and Games to Stimulate Students' Thinking

By Helen H. Moore

SCHOLASTIC PROFESSIONAL BOOKS

New York ● Toronto ● London ● Auckland ● Sydney

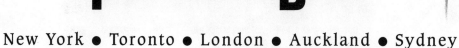

To Carmen, finally.

Acknowledgments

If it's true that our parents are our first teachers, then my first teacher was a lulu. My mother was an inveterate puzzle poser who constantly exhorted my brother and sister and me to "make your own fun!"

I have vivid memories of her asking me, a little-too-innocently, things like, "Which is correct to say: The yolk of an egg **is** white, or the yolk of an egg **are** white?"

"**Is** white, of course," I'd reply, which would set her grinning.

"Wrong," she'd announce. "The yolk of an egg is yellow!"

G-r-r-r-r-r-r.

My mother taught me that it's fun to "just think." She never finished high school, yet she taught me to read before I was five years old. Every day now, events occur that bring to mind some perfectly true and applicable "saying" of hers: Her proverbs and folk wisdom taught me what metaphor and analogy are all about. Her puzzles and jokes exercised my mind in a childhood without 57 channels or Nintendo, and where there was never enough for me to read. There is a lot of her in this book, and in me.

So let me acknowledge my mother, who taught me that although Constantinople is, indeed, a very big word, you can spell it with only two letters: I-T.

Thanks to Terry Cooper of Scholastic Professional Books, and to my husband, Carmen R. Sorvillo, teacher, artist, and solver of puzzles. Vincent Ceci added his special expertise, for which I want to thank him, too.

A very special thank-you also goes to Virginia Dooley, my editor, without whose hard work this book would still be a pile of pages sitting on my desk!

Designed by Vincent Ceci and Drew Hires
Cover and interior illustrations by Rick Brown
Cover design by Vincent Ceci
ISBN 0-590-49795-2

Table of Contents

Introduction

As every teacher knows, a classroom composed of a teacher and twenty or so students quickly begins to resemble a family. (Hopefully, a functional one!) This was really brought home to me every time one of my students would wave a hand in the air for my attention and, without thinking, call me "Ma." And as in any family, it's the sharing of positive experiences, like field trips and parties, school plays and book fairs, that helps the members bond in a fun way. Playing games and solving puzzles together are also great ways to achieve this bond.

I hope you'll find something here that you can use in a way that suits your individual teaching style as well as your students' needs. Following are some more thoughts on ways to use this book.

◆ You may want to make a practice of copying a puzzle onto the board as a "do-now" or a "morning message." Invite students to take copies of puzzles home, to involve parents in finding the solution. You may wish to ask parents to contribute puzzles *they* enjoy.

◆ Even in the most well-organized classroom, emergencies can arise: an assembly is canceled and a block of time may open up, not enough for a formal or even a mini-lesson, but plenty for a worthwhile activity. Or a substitute teacher must be called in for a day or more, and you need to be prepared with activities that require no planning and minimal materials. Having a store of mind-exercising activities on hand makes managing these unexpected openings in your schedule easy. The activities in this book will help.

◆ Learning centers need to contain lots of materials for students to choose from, to reinforce the thinking skills called for in completing the center, and many of the activities in this book are ideal.

◆ In classes grouped heterogeneously, there may be one or more students who always seem to finish assignments "early" or who need a little more of a challenge. Invite such students to try some of these brain-boosters.

◆ You may want to stimulate creative thinking, teaching students that a question may have more than one "correct" answer. Many of the games in this book, like "Categories" or "There Once Was a Cat," demonstrate this.

Some teachers like activities that students can complete more or less independently, while others prefer to work closely with their students on in-class activities. Once you've "walked" your students through the initial activity in a section, you can give them as much or as little guidance as feels comfortable to you. In general, I think students will benefit most if these activities are incorporated into your lessons and taught in the context of your curriculum. A curriculum area is suggested for each activity or game.

Always, when guiding students through the solution to a brain-booster, invite them to "think about their thinking." Encourage them to discover that there can be many ways of reaching the "correct" solution. Students may want to create their own puzzles, games, and brain-boosters to share with you and each other. If they do, you can encourage them and ask how they will incorporate the pattern used in solving the book's puzzle in creating their own. Let them talk, think, and write about their thinking. What did they notice? What was fun? What was difficult? What do they think?

An Important Note: Many students *enjoy* competing against others or against the clock in solving puzzles and playing games. On the other hand, it's probably true that an equal number of students, particularly those with learning disabilities, become nervous when they face a time limit, or any form of competition that calls on the very skills they have such difficulty with. Since one of our purposes in playing games in the classroom is to have fun, we will defeat that purpose if we put undue pressures on these children.

One way to ensure that students feel less pressured might be to invite them to decide on a suitable time limit themselves, if you and they feel a time limit would add something to the activity.

You are the expert on your own students and the best judge of how competitive to make these games. If you feel that setting a time limit or competing in teams would create problems, then by all means use cooperative techniques and lessen competition. The choice is yours.

Part One
Just Think!

For many of the activities in this section, you can either read the instructions aloud to students, write the instructions on the board, or do a combination of the two. Some of the pages are meant to be reproduced for your students to use. Whichever way you use these pages, you will want to model the process for the students before having them attempt to solve the puzzle or play the game themselves. Select the first question and "walk" the students through it.

There Once Was a Cat...

Prepare students by telling them this is an activity for which they'll need to take turns. Start by inviting the class to join you in clapping rhythmically as you recite, "There once was a cat, a (blank) cat." The word you use to fill in the blank should start with the letter a. The next person to recite fills in the blank with a "b" word, then the next person uses a "c" word, and so on.

For example:

There once was a cat, an awful cat.

There once was a cat, a bold cat.

There once was a cat, a calico cat.

There once was a cat, a dainty cat.

Extension:

For an additional challenge, each student may repeat from memory all the words in correct order that those who played before him or her filled in. For example:

There once was a cat, an awful, bold, calico, dainty, cat.

And so on.

A, My Name is Anna

Invite students to take turns changing the final words of each line of the sentence below. The first student must select words that begin with a, the second with b, the third with c, and so on. (See the examples below.)

(Words to be changed are in **bold face**.)

A, my name is **Anna**
and my husband's name is **Al**,
we come from **Alabama**,
and we sell **apples**.

B, my name is **Brett**
and my husband's name is **Bob**,
we come from **Bermuda**,
and we sell **bread**.

Note:
Any other relationship word can be substituted for "husband."

9

Categories

There are many ways to play categorizing games; here is an easy one. (See pages 11-16 for another way.) You can select a topic from the following list and write it on the board. Invite students to work individually, in small groups, or as a class to brainstorm as many items as they can that fit within the category. Set a time limit for a more exciting challenge.

◆ something you eat

◆ an animal

◆ a vegetable

◆ a metal

◆ an item of furniture

◆ a form of transportation

◆ a word that begins with x, q, or z

◆ a dessert

◆ some kind of tool

◆ an item of clothing

◆ a language

◆ a team sport

◆ an individual sport

◆ something made of plastic

◆ something made of wood

◆ something made of metal

◆ a fruit

◆ a flower

◆ a famous building

◆ a geographical feature of the earth

◆ something in a medicine cabinet

◆ something you can ride

◆ an animal with fur

◆ an animal with feathers

◆ an animal with a beak

◆ an animal with claws

◆ an animal with scales

◆ a food you can eat with the skin on

◆ a sound made by an explosion

◆ something rough

◆ something smooth

◆ something wet

◆ something dry

◆ something you need to take care of a baby

Extension:

When students have exhausted this list, invite them to develop categories of their own. They may notice that the above categories can be further subdivided to generate more categories.

Super Categories

Do the activities on pages 12-16 after the activity on page 10, so that students are familiar with the idea of the Category Game. Make and distribute copies of each page, one at a time, as needed.

   To start, invite students to select a letter of the alphabet and ask them to write it in the second column. Students can then work in teams or individually to add as many entries as possible in the third column that fit the category listed in the first column and that start with the initial they've selected.

Example:

Column 1	Column 2	Column 3
something in a classroom	g	girls, globe, gerbil (class pet)...

When they have finished, students should have fun sharing their answers. Accept all answers that students can support with an explanation—"stretching" the category to come up with creative answers is part of the fun of the game. Students can use thumb-up, thumb-down voting to decide whether they accept another student's answer. You can be the final arbiter, to ensure fairness.

Note:
If you decide to make this a contest, it's fun to ascribe point values for finishing, and for having listed entries that no other team or individual has thought of.

11

Super Categories

Choose a letter from the alphabet for column 2. Then list as many entries as possible in Column 3 that match the description in Column 1, and start with the letter in Column 2.

Column 1	Column 2	Column 3
something slippery		
an occupation		
a geographical feature of the earth		
something you wear		
something you cook		
a city of the world		
a toy		
an animal		
a boy's name		
something in an attic		
a girl's name		
something old		
a cartoon character		
something you'd find at the circus		
a mathematical term		

More to do: Think up a category of your own.

Super Categories 2

Choose a letter from the alphabet for column 2. Then list as many entries as possible in Column 3 that match the description in Column 1, and start with the letter in Column 2.

Column 1	Column 2	Column 3
a musical instrument		
a bird		
a wild animal		
a type of transportation		
something you slice		
something you wear		
something you read		
a precious gem		
a type of leader or ruler		
an industry		
a body of water		
a city in Europe		
a green vegetable		
a container		
an animal that lives in water		

More to do: Explain to a friend how you come up with answers. What steps do you follow?

Super Categories 3

Choose a letter from the alphabet for column 2. Then list as many entries as possible in Column 3 that match the description in Column 1, and start with the letter in Column 2.

Column 1	Column 2	Column 3
a liquid		
an insect		
something prehistoric		
a breakfast food		
a feeling		
a coin from any country's currency		
a flower		
a city in North America		
a sport		
a school activity		
a movie star		
something you'd find in a kitchen		
a type of dog		
an author		
a video game		

More to do: Play Super Categories at home with your family or friends. Is it easy to explain what to do?

Super Categories 4

Choose a letter from the alphabet for column 2. Then list as many entries as possible in Column 3 that match the description in Column 1, and start with the letter in Column 2.

Column 1	Column 2	Column 3
something you'd find in outer space		
something loud		
a form of transportation		
something you'd find under the sea		
something nutritious		
something you'd find in a science lab		
something you'd find on a farm		
something you'd find in a hospital		
an animal's habitat		
a book title		
a character in a movie		
a famous artist		
a game		
something you'd find in a garden		
a vegetable that grows under ground		

More to Do: Make up a story using all the entries you suggested for one category.

Super Categories 5

Choose a letter from the alphabet for column 2. Then list as many entries as possible in Column 3 that match the description in Column 1, and start with the letter in Column 2.

Column 1	Column 2	Column 3
a special day in a person's life		
a kind of shop in a mall		
something a teenager likes to do		
something cold		
something people do on vacation		
a book title		
a fruit with more than one seed		
something you'd find on a restaurant menu		
something that has a shell		
something a teacher uses		
something you'd find in a library		
a famous American		
something you'd eat for dessert		
an athlete		
a country		

More to Do: Try this out on your friends and family: read them the entries you've come up with for a category and ask them to guess what the category is.

Going on a Picnic

Tell the class that you are going on a picnic, and they have to figure out what rule you use in determining what to bring. Then say something like, "My name is Ms. /Mr. (fill in your name) and I'm going on a picnic with my class. I think I'll take: (blank)." Then name a food or picnic item that begins with the initial of your name. Turn to the first student and ask what they will bring, saying, for example, "Danielle, what will you bring?"

Danielle: "Uh, I think I'll bring potato chips."
You: "Mmm— no, I don't think we need potato chips...
Makiko, what will you bring?"
Makiko: "I guess I'll bring marshmallows."
You: "Yes, marshmallows would be good...
Evan, what will you bring?"
Evan: "Cookies!"
You: "We don't need cookies."

Continue after this fashion, saying no to children who choose items that don't begin with their initial, and yes to those who do. Invite students to hazard guesses as to what your criterion is for including items, until eventually one student guesses.

Note:

This is a great game to play while riding on a bus for a field trip!

Extension:

Invite students to invent their own guessing games of this type, and play them with their families or friends. Discuss the results.

I Spy

Students take turns giving clues and guessing the identity of items in a given area (e.g., the classroom, the gymnasium, the library). The clues are the initials of the item. Start by saying something like this:

"I spy, with my little eye, something in the classroom that begins with BB."
Invite them to guess, by calling out, raising their hands, or taking turns according to seating, what it is that you spy.

Sample guesses:

"**B**lack **b**oard!"
"No-o-o-o-o!"
"**B**rown **b**ag (for lunch)!"
"Good guess, but that's not what I spy..."
"**B**ig **B**ooks!"
"Yes! That's it! You guessed it!'

The student who guessed correctly gets to "spy" next.

Notes:

◆ Encourage students to be creative; "DW" for "dirty windows" is more challenging than just "w" for windows.
◆ "Spies" may wish to "allow" guesses that do not match what they originally intended as the correct answer, providing the guesser can creatively justify the guess. Some guesses may be so creative the class may wish to award them "correct" status by acclamation or vote.
◆ This game is also lots of fun to play on class trips; students can "spy" unusual items on the bus or out of its windows.

Animal, Vegetable, Mineral

In this classroom version of an old favorite game, students guess the identity of an item by analyzing the answers to a series of "yes" or "no" questions.

Invite one child to choose an object. Once that child is ready, the rest of the students can take turns asking her questions to determine the identity of the object. You may wish to have this child sit near you while the game is being played in case she wants to confer with you before answering a question. There are a few rules that help the game proceed in an orderly way:

◆ Students must raise their hands and be recognized before answering: calling out answers creates too much confusion.

◆ Each student can ask one question at a time, and after receiving an answer, must wait until one other student has asked a question before asking another.

◆ The only acceptable questions are those that can only be answered "yes" or "no."

◆ You may wish to limit the number of questions to twenty, since this game is sometimes known by the name of "Twenty Questions." (The reason it is also known as Animal, Vegetable, Mineral, is that sometimes these three categories form the basis of the first questions asked— you may wish to explain this to students and encourage them to take advantage of this method of narrowing down the amount of information they must elicit.)

◆ The first student to guess the correct answer wins. However, when a student thinks she knows the correct answer, she must announce this as she is recognized. At this time, other students who feel they also know the answer can then write it on a slip of paper along with their name, and fold it shut. The first student can give her answer, and if her answer is correct, she shares credit with all others who also wrote the correct answers on their papers. You and the students may wish to make it a rule that all those who guess, whether verbally or on paper, are henceforward eliminated from play: taking a guess, therefore, entails a risk. If they guess wrong, students have to sit out the rest of the game.

◆ If the guesser is wrong, play continues until the next student who feels ready to, guesses. Follow the same steps as above, to allow all those who think they know the answer to have a chance to share credit.

◆ The winner(s) is (are) the first to guess correctly.

Note:
You may wish to invite students to think of ways to make this into a team game.

Extension:
Ask students if hearing the answers to their classmates' questions helped them. Ask them to explain how. Invite students to reflect on the strategies they used to devise the questions that gave them the most information.

Follow All Directions

In this funny activity, students will practice following oral and written directions. Make enough copies of page 21 for your class and distribute them. Invite students to read and follow all the directions on this page, but say that before they begin doing anything, they must read **all** the directions on the page. Since the last statement tells them not to follow any of the other directions, any children who have not followed your directions will learn the importance of listening to and following directions in an amusing way.

Extension:
Invite your students to create a story or play in which a character gets into difficulties because he or she doesn't listen carefully to directions.

Palindromes

Palindromes are words, sentences, or numbers that read the same way forward and backward. You can use them to introduce new vocabulary, stimulate interest in word games, provide students with new material for writing, or just have fun with these funny words and sentences. Copy and distribute page 22 and guide students in reading the introductory material. Invite them to use the list of palindrome words and helpers to make palindrome sentences in their writing.

Follow All Directions

1. Write your name at the top of this page.

2. Write the name of your school after your name.

3. Stand up next to your chair and stretch your arms overhead.

4. Turn to the person next to you and shake his or her hand

   while saying, "Hi!"

5. Clap your hands three times.

6. Poke a hole in this page with your pencil.

7. Bark once like a dog.

8. Scratch your head with your left hand, while you pat your

   stomach with your right hand.

9. Jump up and spin around.

10. Do not follow the directions in 1-9.

Palindromes

A *palindrome* is a word, sentence, or number that reads the same way forward and backward. They are enjoyed by people of all ages who like to have some fun with words. Some famous palindromes are:

Madam, I'm Adam. (What the first man might have said to the first woman.)
Step on no Pets. (Good advice for animal lovers!)
A man, a plan, a canal, Panama! (Research challenge: find out what this palindrome has to do with a President of the United States.)

Use the palindromic words and helpers below to write a palindrome sentence on the other side of this page.

Palindromic Words

Mom	dud
Dad	sees
pop	radar
noon	Anna
level	deed
Otto	toot
eve	eye
peep	nun
pep	mum
ewe	did
did	radar
kayak	madam
Bob	hah
tot	ma'am

Palindrome Helpers

These words can be read backwards to form new words. They can be helpful when you want to make a palindrome.

but	reed	spat
no	leg	span
not	sleek	step
saw	strap	reward
yam	tar	cod
mood	top	emit
live	stop	sloop
Noel	sleep	slap
now	sinned	keep
net	stab	
draw	star	

More to Do: Try writing a story whose main character speaks in palindromes, or a mystery in which a palindrome might provide a clue.

Spoonerisms

A *spoonerism* is something like a Freudian slip—a slip of the tongue that often reveals more meaning (or at least a funnier meaning) than the speaker intended.

It's a swapping of the initial sounds (in phonetic terms, the *onsets*) of two words to create two different words. Spoonerisms were named after W. A. Spooner, an Englishman who was a notorious bird watcher—actually, he was a notorious *word botcher*. He was Dean and Warder of New College at Oxford University, and lived from 1844-1930.

Discuss Spooner and his spoonerisms with students. Put one or two of the following spoonerisms on the board and invite students to determine what Spooner meant to say. They may enjoy recognizing spoonerisms when they hear them in speeches or on live television shows.

What he said:

a. In a sermon, Spooner said, "Yes, Our Lord is a shoving leopard."

b. In another sermon, he said, "Which of us has not felt in his heart a half-warmed fish?"

c. To a flunking, lazy student, he said, "Sir, you have tasted a whole worm. You have hissed my mystery lectures."

What he meant:

a. Yes, Our Lord is a loving shepherd.

b. Which of us has not felt in his heart a half-formed wish?

c. Sir, you have wasted a whole term. You have missed my history lectures.

Extensions:

◆ Have students create funny spoonerisms of their own,
◆ Have students find out more about Spooner. Ask them to present reports about him and his spoonerisms.
◆ Students may want to research Oxford University and create an Oxford display for the classroom.
◆ Suggest that students work in small groups to write a play about someone whose spoonerisms cause funny misunderstandings.

Analogies

Analogies are used in everyday life, in teaching, and in testing. They're fun to do, and once you guide students through the first few on this list, they should have fun figuring out the rest.

Students find it easy to figure out analogies once they realize that analogies are all about relationships. To guide students through the first few samples, below, have them think about the relationship between the first two items named,

For example, in the following analogy: *hot* is to *cold* as *in* is to_____, the relationship between *hot* and *cold* is one of opposites. Elicit this from students, then invite them to guess what the opposite of *in* is. Of course, it's *out*. So, the analogy is **hot** is to **cold** as **in** is to **out**.

Here are other common relationships used in analogies. You and your students may enjoy thinking of others.

SYNONYMS *silk* is to *smooth* as *sandpaper* is to *rough* (see 13, 15, below)
PART TO WHOLE *finger* is to *hand* as *toe* is to *foot* (see 6, 14, below)
PURPOSE *chair* is to *sit* as *bed* is to *sleep* (see 16, 17, 20, below)
CAUSE AND EFFECT *eating* is to *satisfaction* as *starving* is to *hunger* (see 5, below)
DEGREE *pretty* is to *beautiful* as *cool* is to *cold* (see 15, below)
CHARACTERISTICS *pepper* is to *spicy* as *oatmeal* is to *bland* (see 11, below)
PLACE *airplane* is to *sky* as *boat* is to *sea* (see 1, below)

Invite your students to complete the analogies at right. You can read them aloud or write them on the board. (The notation : :: : is commonly used to denote " is to, as, is to".)

Extensions:

Invite students to discuss the relationships between the parts of an analogy. Accept all reasonable answers. Suggest that students create their own analogies.

		Answers:	
1.	car : garage :: coat :	1.	closet
2.	dog : bark:: bird :	2.	chirps/tweets
3.	one: two :: three :	3.	six
4.	she : her :: he :	4.	him
5.	happiness : laughter :: sadness :	5.	tears/crying
6.	knee : leg :: elbow :	6.	arm
7.	girl : mother :: boy	7.	father
8.	left : right :: top	8.	bottom
9.	car : driver :: plane :	9.	pilot
10.	rich : wealth :: sick :	10.	health
11.	green : color :: cinnamon :	11.	flavor
12.	coffee : drink :: hamburger :	12.	eat
13.	easy : simple :: hard :	13.	difficult
14.	page : book :: Spain :	14.	Europe
15.	small : tiny :: big :	15.	large/huge/gigantic
16.	swim : pool :: jog :	16.	road/street
17.	glove : hand :: shoe:	17.	foot
18.	breakfast : dinner :: morning :	18.	evening
19.	blue : color :: round :	19.	shape
20.	date : calendar :: time :	20.	watch/clock

Limericks

Although some of the limericks most people are familiar with are not suitable for class-room use, this is a clever literary form that is very satisfying to write and to recite.

A limerick has five lines; lines 1, 2, and 5 contain three beats and rhyme with each other, and lines 3 and 4 contain two beats and rhyme.

The most famous of all limerick writers is Edward Lear. Born in England in 1812, Lear was the 21st of 22 children. He is famous for his wonderful nonsensical rhymes and stories, including the "Father William" limericks, the Nonsense Alphabet, and *The Owl and the Pussycat*. Lear wrote the following limerick:

There was an Old Lady whose folly,
Induced her to sit on a holly,
Whereon, by a thorn,
Her dress being torn,
She quickly became melancholy.

After introducing your students to the limerick form and to Edward Lear, invite them to write their own limericks. The starters below can be helpful. You may want to under-line the stressed syllables to make them easier for the students to identify.

There **was** a young **woman** named **Sue,**   (line 1, rhymes with 2 and 5)
Who **said,** "I don't **know** what to **do**;"   (line 2, rhymes with 1 and 5)
She **looked** up and **sighed**,   (line 3, rhymes with line 4)
            (line 4)
            (line 5)

There **once** was a **fellow** named **Jack,**   (line 1, rhymes with 2 and 5)
Whose **clothing** was **worn** front-to-**back**,   (line 2, rhymes with 1 and 5)
When **asked** why this **was**,   (line 3, rhymes with line 4)
            (line 4)
            (line 5)

It's Not What You Say...

...it's how you say it. If you've ever doubted the truth of that statement, play this word game with your students. Students will enjoy exploring the differences that intonation makes to meaning.

Write the first sentence below on the board. Invite students to take turns reading the sentences aloud, emphasizing a different word each time (see below). Discuss the meaning of each reading with them.

1. **I** did not say you broke my yellow pen.
2. I **did** not say you broke my yellow pen.
3. I did **not** say you broke my yellow pen.
4. I did not **say** you broke my yellow pen.
5. I did not say **you** broke my yellow pen.
6. I did not say you **broke** my yellow pen.
7. I did not say you broke **my** yellow pen.
8. I did not say you broke my **yellow** pen.
9. I did not say you broke my yellow **pen**.

Suggested Meanings:
1. I didn't say it, someone else did.
2. I did not say it, and don't you say I did!
3. I did **not** say it, and you'd better stop saying I did!
4. I may have **suspected** it, but I didn't say it.
5. Someone broke it. Not necessarily you.
6. You did **something** to it!
7. Someone else says you broke theirs!
8. You broke my other pen.
9. You broke something else of mine that is yellow.

Extensions:

Invite students to create their own sentences that can change meaning depending on the intonation. Your students may wish to write and perform a play featuring a character who causes problems by emphasizing the wrong words when she speaks, or in which confusion is created by a written note which contains all the correct words, but not the same emphasis as a spoken sentence.

Pass the Poem, Please

This game was invented by a French poet named Dulos in 1648. The rules are simple: Each player writes four words on a page. These become the final, rhyming words of a four-line verse (a, a, b, b).
For example:

kid
lid
car
far

A possible poem that can be created from these words might be:

**There was a kid,
Who flipped his lid.
He drove his car
Much, much too far.**

Introduce students to the form and model the above poem for them. Guide the whole group in writing one or two collaboratively.

Note:
Decide in advance whether you want to have a time limit. You can play as many three-, four-, or five-minute rounds as you wish.

Fun fact:
Poetry contests similar to this have been popular in many Asian and European countries for many years.

SURVIVE!

Inviting students to imagine a scenario in which they will be isolated for an indeterminate period of time, in a location without many amenities, can lead to a lot of creative thinking and be a springboard to many activities. A desert island, a space station on the moon, or a remote mountain top, for example, can be the locations for imaginations to go to work!

After selecting a location, students should think about several things. First, they should work together to brainstorm a list of the natural resources they think might exist at the location. Then they may ask themselves questions like the following:

Where am I?

What are the physical characteristics of this place?

How did I get here?

Am I alone?

Am I with a group?

Any chance of my/our leaving or being rescued anytime soon?

If I'm/we're going to be here a while, what will I/we need to survive (food and shelter)? (This question may lead to an interesting digression about what is necessary to support life, what the differences are between needs and wants, and so on.)

Once I've/we've decided on my/our survival needs, think: Does this site have these necessities?

Should I/we expend my/our energies on survival, or on getting back home/being rescued?

What is the climate?

What kind of shelter can I/we build?

What kinds of inventions might I/we create to make life easier?

What things will I miss? books? video games? What will replace them?

What will I/we eat? How will the food be prepared?

What if I'm not rescued for a long time—maybe years…. If there are others here with me, what kind of society might evolve? If I'm here alone, what kind of person might I become?

Notes:

Students may be interested in researching real-life examples of survival, like the one depicted in the movie, *Alive!* Or they may want to read about fictional adventures like that of *Robinson Crusoe* by Daniel Defoe, or, depending on their ages and interests, watch the more fanciful Disney film, *Swiss Family Robinson*.

Extensions:

Students can use the brainstormed lists to work collaboratively or individually on a play, story, poem, or song about the experiences they've postulated. They may wish to create models of the shelter and inventions they've envisioned.

Rhyme Time

What would you call a piece of pasta in the shape of a dog? A Poodle Noodle, maybe? How about a rabbit's dinner that is given, instead, to a bird? A Parrot Carrot? A place for a married man to hang his hat and coat? How about a Hubby Cubby?

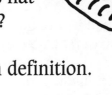

Think of a two-word rhyme and a fun definition. Then illustrate your rhyme below.

Is *That* a Fact?

Present the following statements to students either verbally or by writing them on the board. Ask them to decide if the statement is fact or opinion. You may want to model the process by saying something like, "A human being cannot live long without food. Fact or opinion?" (Fact) Contrast this with an opinion by saying, "A human being cannot live long without pizza." (Opinion, although if your students are typical, they may dispute this, pizza being by far the favorite food of American students (fact).) Ask students to explain their answers.

1. Asia contains more than half of the world's population. (fact)
2. Crowded cities are the worst places to live. (opinion)
3. The faces of four U.S. presidents are carved into Mt. Rushmore. (fact)
4. Up to 100,000 workers labored for five years to create one pyramid in Egypt. (fact)
5. *Gone With the Wind* is the best movie ever made. (opinion)
6. The deepest lake in the U.S. is in Oregon. (fact)
7. The Great Wall of China is the greatest construction feat humans have ever accomplished. (opinion)
8. *Schindler's List* won the Oscar for Best Picture of 1993. (fact)
9. In Argentina it is winter during June, July, and August. (fact)
10. If the Earth's orbit were 1% farther from the sun, all of our water would have frozen about 2 billion years ago. (fact)
11. The Aztecs were a cruel and warlike people. (opinion)
12. Miranda is a beautiful name. (opinion)
13. Skateboarding is fun. (opinion)
14. A carrot is a vegetable. (fact)
15. Unleaded gasoline makes cars run better. (opinion)
16. Hamburgers taste better than chicken. (opinion)
17. Blood makes a complete trip through the body in under 25 seconds. (fact)
18. John F. Kennedy was the greatest president in U.S. history. (opinion)
19. June is Zoo and Aquarium Month. (fact)
20. Beethoven, Hayden, and Mozart are the world's greatest musicians. (opinion)

Extension:

Newspapers contain a blend of fact and opinion-based stories. Generally, the hard news section in the front of the paper is all news and usually contains only facts. The features section is full of human interest stories, which blend facts and opinion, as do the editorials and the letters to the editor. You may wish to invite students to read the local papers and look for examples of facts and opinions. (Many newspapers have speakers' bureaus which will provide an editor or reporter to speak to your class. Some offer tours to school groups, and there are over 700 newspapers across the United States and Canada that offer Newspaper in Education programs, with free teaching materials. Call your local paper for more information.)

What's In A Name?

Here's a silly way for your students to create the perfect name for a rock band. Have them use the lists of words on page 32. Have them select one word from each column and put the three words together to create a great name!

Invite students to think about what makes this game work. Elicit that naming words are nouns, and words that describe nouns can be other nouns or adjectives.
All the words in the first column are adjectives, the second column contains a combination of adjectives and nouns, and the words in the third column are exclusively nouns. Encourage students to collect funny names of popular bands, and analyze them in terms of parts of speech.

Extensions:

Collect interesting adjectives and nouns contributed by students on a "word wall" or in a learning center. Categorize the words by part of speech. When pre-writing poetry, have students randomly pick one adjective and one noun, and write a brief verse starting with the two words they've chosen. (Add a verb and an adverb and call it an "instant poem.") This is a great way to limber up the poetry muscles and jump-start students' imaginations!

Name _____

What's In A Name?

Here's a great way to choose a name for a rock band. Just choose one word from each column and put them together in order. Then sit back and wait for the record company executives to come calling!

blonde	watermelon	roosters
dangerous	crayon	cavemen
hairy	pumpkin	dumplings
shining	colorful	groundhogs
tiny	informative	parakeets
barking	winter	hedgehogs
teenage	flower	club
permanent	watery	shutter bugs
international	young	warriors
misunderstood	football	masterminds
animated	robot	presidents
tyrannical	soapy	moonbeams
ancient	wrinkled	infants
happy	morning	cartoons
flexible	motorized	scholars

More to Do: Think about the order of the words.
Does this work if you change the order? Why or why not?

Riddle Me This...

These riddles are easy to solve if your students think of homographs. Put one on the board every morning for a fun "do now" or ask the questions verbally for a guessing game.

1. What does a homerun hitter's tool have in common with a small, furry, flying mammal? (They're both bats.)
2. baseball player/cake mix (batter)
3. bird's nose/statement of money owed (bill)
4. eat oatmeal out of it/game of ten pins (bowl)
5. card game/road over water (bridge)
6. make weary/dig a hole (bore)
7. sound a dog makes/tree covering (bark)
8. male deer/dollar bill (buck)
9. to cut/ to fasten (clip)
10. something you chew/part of the body that helps you chew (gum)
11. large wild bird/to lower, suddenly (duck)
12. month, day, year/ small, sweet fruit (date)
13. what a queen or king does to a nobleman/ add sound to a film (dub)
14. a showing of science projects/ just, right (fair)
15. a stroke of luck in game/ a type of fish (fluke)
16. a blacksmith's tool/move ahead forcefully (forge)
17. a part of a cemetery/ something very serious (grave)
18. to keep out of sight/an animal skin (hide)
19. a false statement/ to place one's body in a flat position (lie)
20. breakfast, lunch, or dinner/ ground grain (meal)
21. unkind/average (mean)
22. a dark spot on the skin/a small underground animal (mole)
23. a long piece of wood/either end of the earth's axis (pole)
24. to hold back/ part of a song (refrain)
25. the end point of a stick/an extra amount of money given for services (tip)

Extension:
Some of the words above have an additional meaning. Ask students if they can think of another meaning to add to any of the riddles.

Part Two

Mental Math Mysteries and Picture Puzzles

Many of the activities in this section are contained on reproducible pages. Simply copy, distribute, and invite students to work singly, in groups, or as a class to complete. You may wish to send the pages home for students to share with their families.

Secret Number

Some of these games have been around for years, but they still provoke oooohs and aaaahs when students encounter them for the first time. Walk through one example with the class, then invite students to try them on their own. Ask if anyone can figure out the principles that make this work.

1. Think of a number (but don't tell). ———→ *Say, for example, 8.*

2. Double it. ———→ *8+8=16*

3. Add 14. ———→ *16+14=30*

4. Divide by 2. ———→ *30/2=15*

5. Take away the first number you thought of. → *15-8=7*

6. The answer is 7.

Extension:
Once they've figured out the "secret," invite students to experiment with the formula. How many steps can they add? What needs to happen in order to guarantee that the questioner always has control of the information necessary to know the answer?

Name _____

Connect the Dots

Play this game with a partner. Take turns drawing horizontal or vertical (but no diagonal) lines between any two dots. When you draw the line that completes a box, put your initial in that box, and take another turn. When all the dots have been connected, count the number of boxes with your initials. The player with the most boxes is the winner.

More to do: Is there a "secret" to getting the most boxes? Is it like tic-tac-toe? Think about the strategy that seems to ensure you will win the most boxes. Can you put it into words?

Who's Got the Pen?

If you have seven white pens and six black pens, and you cut them apart and shuffle them around, you've still got seven white pens and six black pens, haven't you? Not in this puzzle!

Copy and distribute page 38. Ask students to count the number of pens, noting how many are black and how many are white. Then invite them to cut the page apart along the cut lines. This will produce three strips of paper, a long one with all the point ends on it, and two short ones with the bottom ends of the pens on them. Show students how to realign the three sections, switching the bottom two (see diagram at right). Now invite them to count the black and white pens. There are now six white and seven black!

Invite students to investigate what causes the switch. There are still thirteen pens illustrated, so where did the white one go? And where did the black one come from?

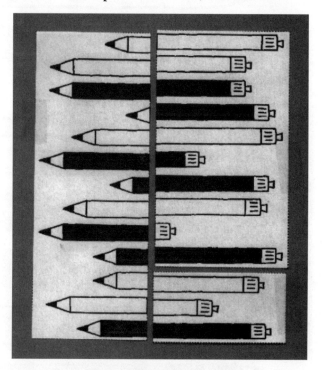

Extension:
Students may enjoy making their own versions of this puzzle once they've figured out what makes it work.

This Won't Fly...or Will It?

This puzzle provides practice in solving problems. Distribute copies of page 39 to each student. Ask students to cut the shapes apart along the heavy solid lines. Then ask them to arrange the pieces to form the word "fly." This isn't as easy as it sounds! To help students "see" the solution, they can place the light-colored letters against a dark background. This is a great way to introduce students in an art class to the idea of negative and positive space.

Name _____

Who's Got the Pen?

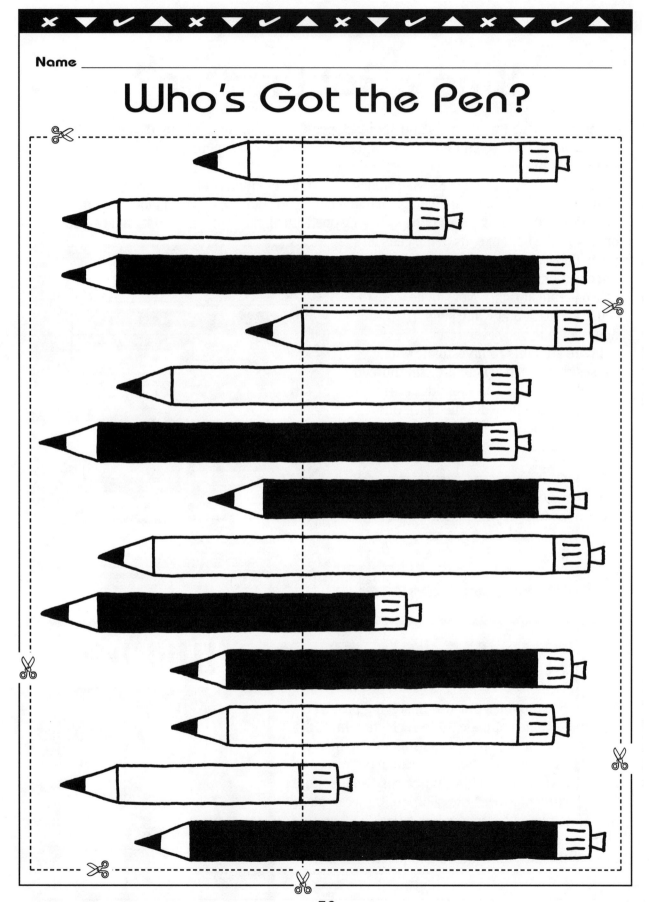

Name _____

This Won't Fly...or Will It?

Can you cut out and rearrange the shapes below to form the word *fly*?

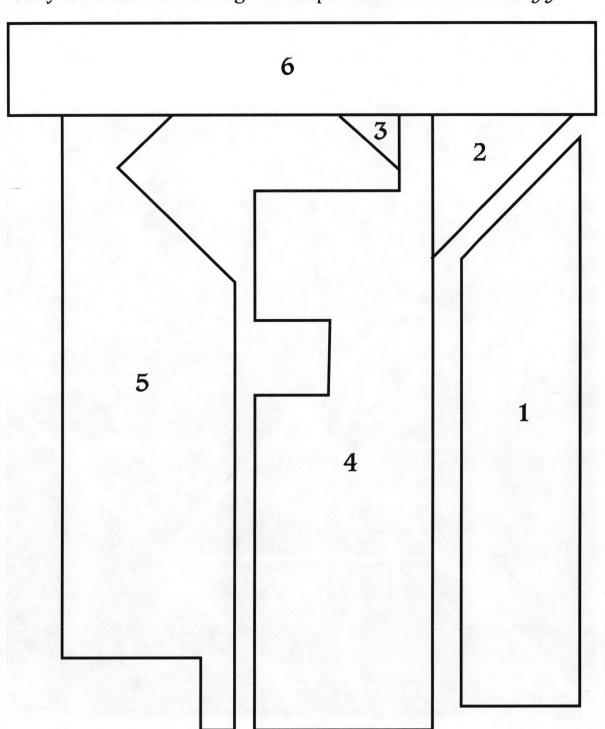

A Tangram

There's no right or wrong way to "do" a tangram—that's what makes them fun for all kinds of thinkers. Duplicate and distribute the tangram shape below. (You may want students to trace their tangram onto cardboard before cutting it out.) Encourage students to experiment with tangrams, finding the many shapes that can be made out of the original seven. It seems like it should be easy to put the shapes back together into a square once they have been cut apart, but it's not always so.

What's Wrong With This Picture?

The "What's Wrong With This Picture" puzzles on the following pages are simple to do. Students study the pictures and decide what's missing. They can write the answer at the bottom of the page, or share their answers aloud during a class discussion.

Answers are:

Page 42:
no receiver on phone
manhole without cover
upside down plane
upside down surfer
beach instead of street
party blower instead of whistle
upside down building in water

Page 44:
no cross strings on racket
football helmet on tennis player
stripes going wrong way on flag
no pole for umbrella
baseball instead of tennis ball
flipper instead of sneaker

Page 43:
no wheels on car
missing fork tine
upside down door
no doornob
hinges on door in wrong place
missing table leg
no faucet on sink

Page 45:
boat on highway
dog driving truck
square wheel
no pedals on bike
no collar attached to leash
dog walker wearing snorkel
fish in sky

Page 46:
train in sky
missing pontoon on plane
backwards fishing poles
sink in water
upside down oar
elephant in forest
fisherman wearing skates

What's Wrong With This Picture?

What's Wrong With This Picture ?

Name _____

What's Wrong With This Picture?

What's Wrong With This Picture?

What's Wrong With This Picture ?

Part Three
Wacky Wordies

mind
matter

Mind over Matter

Newspaper column

The puzzles in this section are word games with a twist: to solve them it helps to be able to think *visually* and *verbally* at the same time. (Not always as easy as it sounds!)

To play, make and distribute copies to students. (If you are doing a lesson on idioms, or colorful or figurative language, these puzzles can fit in nicely.) Each represents a familiar phrase (or cliché), an expression, or a proverb. Each page contains four boxes with a word or words inside it. The orientation, placement, or appearance of the word inside the box give clues to the solution of the puzzle. See the examples above.

Invite students to work together to solve the first few wacky wordies, and when they get the hang of it, have them try some on their own. (Answers are on page 64.)

Extension:
Encourage interested students to try creating their own wacky wordies for extra fun.

Wacky Wordies

Here are some wacky word puzzles for you to enjoy. They represent everyday expressions or familiar words. To solve them, remember these hints: look at the way the word is placed. Is it up, down, to the right, to the left, or in the center of the box? Look at the way each word is printed: Is the ink light or dark? Is it *over* or *under* another word? Is it *before* or *after* another word? Does it remind you of anything? Let your mind play with the ideas the wordies suggest. And most important—have fun!

DE AL

walk
there

overs
overs
overs
overs
overs
overs
overs

TROUBLE

Wacky Wordies

Here are some more of those wacky word puzzles for you to enjoy. Remember: they represent everyday expressions or familiar words. To solve them, remember these hints: Look at the way the word is placed. Is it up, down, to the right, to the left, or in the center of the box? Look at the way each word printed: Is the ink light or dark? Is it *over* or *under* another word? Is it *before* or *after* another word? Does it remind you of anything? Let your mind play with the ideas the wordies suggest. And most important—have fun.

man
base

feeling

age *beauty*

he's

the hill

Wacky Wordies

Here are some more of those wacky word puzzles for you to enjoy. Remember: they represent everyday expressions or familiar words. To solve them, remember these hints: Look at the way the word is placed. Is it up, down, to the right, to the left, or in the center of the box? Look at the way each word printed: Is the ink light or dark? Is it *over* or *under* another word? Is it *before* or *after* another word? Does it remind you of anything? Let your mind play with the ideas the wordies suggest. And most important—have fun.

pox

a rock

CAUGHT

a hard place

tunnel the light

S
C
H
S C H O O L
O
O
L

Wacky Wordies

Here are some more of those wacky word puzzles for you to enjoy. Remember: they represent everyday expressions or familiar words. To solve them, remember these hints: Look at the way the word is placed. Is it up, down, to the right, to the left, or in the center of the box? Look at the way each word printed: Is the ink light or dark? Is it *over* or *under* another word? Is it *before* or *after* another word? Does it remind you of anything? Let your mind play with the ideas the wordies suggest. And most important—have fun.

**W
I
N
G**

way to skin a cat
way to skin a cat
way to skin a cat
way to skin a cat
WaY to sKIn a Cat
way to skin a cat

Wacky Wordies

Here are some more of those wacky word puzzles for you to enjoy. Remember: they represent everyday expressions or familiar words. To solve them, remember these hints: Look at the way the word is placed. Is it up, down, to the right, to the left, or in the center of the box? Look at the way each word printed: Is the ink light or dark? Is it *over* or *under* another word? Is it *before* or *after* another word? Does it remind you of anything? Let your mind play with the ideas the wordies suggest. And most important—have fun.

hearted

Skating

I C E

a
l
u
m
i
n
u
m

enCOUNTERs

Name _____

Wacky Wordies

Here are some more of those wacky word puzzles for you to enjoy. Remember: they represent everyday expressions or familiar words. To solve them, remember these hints: Look at the way the word is placed. Is it up, down, to the right, to the left, or in the center of the box? Look at the way each word printed: Is the ink light or dark? Is it *over* or *under* another word? Is it *before* or *after* another word? Does it remind you of anything? Let your mind play with the ideas the wordies suggest. And most important—have fun.

s e s a m e

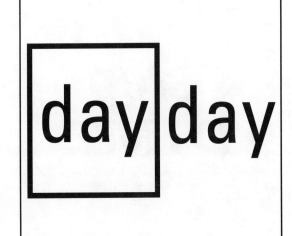

Name _____

Wacky Wordies

Here are some more of those wacky word puzzles for you to enjoy. Remember: they represent everyday expressions or familiar words. To solve them, remember these hints: Look at the way the word is placed. Is it up, down, to the right, to the left, or in the center of the box? Look at the way each word printed: Is the ink light or dark? Is it *over* or *under* another word? Is it *before* or *after* another word? Does it remind you of anything? Let your mind play with the ideas the wordies suggest. And most important—have fun.

chip
his shoulder

all your cards
the table

stop
DIME

The
It's
Bag

Wacky Wordies

Here are some more of those wacky word puzzles for you to enjoy. Remember: they represent everyday expressions or familiar words. To solve them, remember these hints: Look at the way the word is placed. Is it up, down, to the right, to the left, or in the center of the box? Look at the way each word printed: Is the ink light or dark? Is it *over* or *under* another word? Is it *before* or *after* another word? Does it remind you of anything? Let your mind play with the ideas the wordies suggest. And most important—have fun.

hang	put
the jump *lake*	**down** *The Farm*

Name _____

Wacky Wordies

Here are some more of those wacky word puzzles for you to enjoy. Remember: they represent everyday expressions or familiar words. To solve them, remember these hints: Look at the way the word is placed. Is it up, down, to the right, to the left, or in the center of the box? Look at the way each word printed: Is the ink light or dark? Is it *over* or *under* another word? Is it *before* or *after* another word? Does it remind you of anything? Let your mind play with the ideas the wordies suggest. And most important—have fun.

woods woods woods woods woods
woods woods woods woods woods
woods woods woods woods woods
woods woods woods woods woods
woods woods woods woods woods
woods woods woods woods woods
woods woods woods LOST woods
woods woods woods woods woods
woods woods woods woods woods
woods woods woods woods woods
woods woods woods woods woods

T
H
E

P
R
I
C
E

change

skirt

Wacky Wordies

Here are some more of those wacky word puzzles for you to enjoy. Remember: they represent everyday expressions or familiar words. To solve them, remember these hints: Look at the way the word is placed. Is it up, down, to the right, to the left, or in the center of the box? Look at the way each word printed: Is the ink light or dark? Is it *over* or *under* another word? Is it *before* or *after* another word? Does it remind you of anything? Let your mind play with the ideas the wordies suggest. And most important—have fun.

Wacky Wordies

Here are some more of those wacky word puzzles for you to enjoy. Remember: they represent everyday expressions or familiar words. To solve them, remember these hints: Look at the way the word is placed. Is it up, down, to the right, to the left, or in the center of the box? Look at the way each word printed: Is the ink light or dark? Is it *over* or *under* another word? Is it *before* or *after* another word? Does it remind you of anything? Let your mind play with the ideas the wordies suggest. And most important—have fun.

bit	sun
	day day

Wacky Wordies

Here are some more of those wacky word puzzles for you to enjoy. Remember: they represent everyday expressions or familiar words. To solve them, remember these hints: Look at the way the word is placed. Is it up, down, to the right, to the left, or in the center of the box? Look at the way each word printed: Is the ink light or dark? Is it *over* or *under* another word? Is it *before* or *after* another word? Does it remind you of anything? Let your mind play with the ideas the wordies suggest. And most important—have fun.

timetime

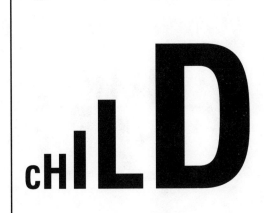

the difference

LOOK

Wacky Wordies

Here are some more of those wacky word puzzles for you to enjoy. Remember: they represent everyday expressions or familiar words. To solve them, remember these hints: Look at the way the word is placed. Is it up, down, to the right, to the left, or in the center of the box? Look at the way each word printed: Is the ink light or dark? Is it *over* or *under* another word? Is it *before* or *after* another word? Does it remind you of anything? Let your mind play with the ideas the wordies suggest. And most important—have fun.

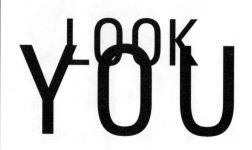

LOOK
YOU

COME SERVED
COME SERVED

and
gloomy

RECORD
RECORD

Wacky Wordies

Here are some more of those wacky word puzzles for you to enjoy. Remember: they represent everyday expressions or familiar words. To solve them, remember these hints: Look at the way the word is placed. Is it up, down, to the right, to the left, or in the center of the box? Look at the way each word printed: Is the ink light or dark? Is it *over* or *under* another word? Is it *before* or *after* another word? Does it remind you of anything? Let your mind play with the ideas the wordies suggest. And most important—have fun.

moon	all the rULEs
dinner the table	stage

Name _____

Wacky Wordies

Here are some more of those wacky word puzzles for you to enjoy. Remember: they represent everyday expressions or familiar words. To solve them, remember these hints: Look at the way the word is placed. Is it up, down, to the right, to the left, or in the center of the box? Look at the way each word printed: Is the ink light or dark? Is it *over* or *under* another word? Is it *before* or *after* another word? Does it remind you of anything? Let your mind play with the ideas the wordies suggest. And most important—have fun.

left *out* field

in *first* **line**

BROTHER

Name _____

Wacky Wordies

Here are some more of those wacky word puzzles for you to enjoy. Remember: they represent everyday expressions or familiar words. To solve them, remember these hints: Look at the way the word is placed. Is it up, down, to the right, to the left, or in the center of the box? Look at the way each word printed: Is the ink light or dark? Is it *over* or *under* another word? Is it *before* or *after* another word? Does it remind you of anything? Let your mind play with the ideas the wordies suggest. And most important—have fun.

LOOK

b e n d
backwards

V**IO**Lᴇᴛ

SISTER

Wacky Wordies Answer Key

Page 48
- square deal *or* big deal
- walk over there
- leftovers
- big trouble

Page 49
- man on base
- feeling down
- age before beauty
- he's over the hill

Page 50
- small pox
- caught between a rock and a hard place
- the light at the end of the tunnel
- school crossing

Page 51
- left wing
- more than one way to skin a cat
- the joke's on me
- vacation break

Page 52
- faint hearted
- skating on thin ice
- aluminum siding
- close encounters

Page 53
- open sesame
- One nation, under God
- double jeopardy
- day in and day out

Page 54
- chip on his shoulder
- putting all your cards on the table
- stop on a dime
- it's in the bag

Page 55
- hang up
- put down
- jump in the lake
- down on the farm

Page 56
- lost in the woods
- the price is right
- small change
- miniskirt

Page 57
- a dark night
- backbend
- new underwear
- around and around in circles

Page 58
- little bit
- sunlight
- waving good-by
- day after day after day

Page 59
- time after time
- a growing child
- splitting the difference
- look to the left

Page 60
- look behind you
- first come, first served
- dark and gloomy
- broken record

Page 61
- moonlight
- breaking all the rules
- dinner on the table
- center stage

Page 62
- out in left field
- big sister
- first in line
- little brother

Page 63
- look to the right
- bend over backwards
- shrinking violet
- little sister